# *Hildreth's* ADVICE *for* MARRIAGE

*Hildreth's*

# ADVICE *for* MARRIAGE

•1891•

WELBECK

Published by Welbeck
An imprint of Welbeck Non-Fiction Limited,
part of Welbeck Publishing Group.
20 Mortimer Street,
London W1T 3JW

First published by J. S. Ogilvie Publishing Company, 1891

This edition published by Welbeck, 2021

A CIP catalogue record for this book is available
from the British Library

ISBN
Hardback - 9781787398689
eBook - 9781787398696

Typeset by EnvyDesignLtd.co.uk
Printed and bound in the UK

10 9 8 7 6 5 4 3 2 1

www.welbeckpublishing.com

"...the tale that I relate
This lesson seems to carry —
Choose not alone a proper mate,
But proper time to marry."

*'Pairing Time Anticipated, Moral' (c. 1794)*
*William Cowper*

# INTRODUCTION

It is not intended to advise against marriage, nor to draw the line too closely as to the don't marry class, but simply to hint at the errors of some persons who match badly on so long a contract. The "yes or no" question is the vital one for all young people to answer. Some answer too soon, others wait too long, others never reach such a climax of happiness as to be invited by an eligible partner. The genius of selection is the rarest of faculties. What most puzzles the will and makes us bear the ills we have is the theme of selection. A mother's or father's view of a suitor may be at variance with the daughter's wish and destroy the peace of both for a lifetime. But quite generally the real trouble arises from a spiteful choice or a hasty one, or one in some of the forms here mentioned. Should these hints prevent one unhappy marriage, they will well repay the little study that their brevity requires.

# ADVICE FOR MARRIAGE

*Don't marry for beauty merely.* Very few have a supply that would last a full dozen years in a married life that should continue for three decades. And, more than that, beauty is not the only requisite to happiness. Very handsome people are almost always vain, often exacting, and generally live on their form, paying little or no attention to the rarer qualities of manhood or womanhood. If one seeks beauty alone, he will find it in the fields and flowers and gardens, in paintings, art works, and things of nature; while the real pleasures of life may be found in a thousand ways outside of the worship of beauty.

There are a dozen considerations beyond beauty that should govern the choice of a companion. Think for a moment whom you admire most, trust implicitly, and love more ardently than all others. Truly, it is not the wax-doll face in a milliner's window; were that so, why not marry the model and get the perfection of beauty? The day will come when the "rain beats in at the heart windows". The time may run along so fast till the summer is over and the winter snow-drifts shade your locks with silver, when one by one of your friends will visit at the fireside, when some one will love you for your mind and heart and nobleness. Some one suited to your silver-age condition and disposition will be beautiful without any name for beauty; as the soldier said of Grant's face, after Shiloh's bloody battle, "That was the handsomest face I ever saw"; yet it was plain and dusty and rugged.

Prize-winners in matrimony have been women of finer mould than mere beauties. Women who have won the hearts of statesmen, and painters and poets, and the good and great of all time, were women of fascination, or what the Southern ladies call sweet women, and not alone noted for their beauty. Many a one has been known to have been plain but social; not always unhandsome, but never beautiful. They are the best wives and noblest mothers who have more to commend them than mere grace of features, shade of skin, or color of eyes, or art of beautifying. Some are frivolous, and more are flattered into danger. The most miserable man I know is married to one of the most beautiful women. He is jealous; she is exposed to insults unawares. Their home is a Hades six days out of seven. I've heard him wish she were less attractive!

❖

*Don't marry a man for money.* If money is your real object, the older and uglier he is, the better; for nothing should come between you and the chosen idol of your affection. If you marry one for his money, he will find it out shortly. What sublime contempt a man must have for one who simply loves his pocket-book! Why not love his farm, or lumber-yard, or herd of cattle? The love of money is a miserly pretence of affection that leads to discontent, distrust, and disgust when they find it out. Besides, wealthy men are men of care. The wife of a noted millionaire has had her husband's body stolen from its vault, has been long kept in agony, is an object of pity to all who know her. Another wife was heard to say, “Why, I don’t have the privilege, nor the money, nor the good times that my girl Bridget enjoys. I am poor and anxious and depressed, and weary of hearing my husband say, over and over again, ‘You are fixing for the poor-house.’ He really thinks and believes we will end life in the poor-house; and yet he enjoys a princely income.” Thousands of such men carry their load of care, and load of wealth, and load of anxiety, and how can they carry any burden of love?

❖

*Don't marry a very small man*—a little fellow far below all proportion; try to get some form to admire, something to shape things to, and some one who is not lost in a crowd completely, who is too little to admire and too small for beauty. You may need strong arms and brave hands to protect you. You will need hands to provide for and maintain you, and a good form is a fine beginning of manhood or womanhood. Mental greatness is not measured by size of brain or bodily proportions. Great men are neither always wise nor always large; they are more often of more medium build, and well balanced in gifts of mental and physical development. Of the two, a very large man is better than a small one, and a medium large woman likewise.

❖

*Don't marry too young.* The right age to marry is a matter of taste; twenty-one for girls, and twenty-four for men may be a little arbitrary, but certainly is sensible. The happy early marriages are rare. It too often happens that love is mistaken, or poorly informed, or lacks an anchor in good judgment. There is no use of reasoning about it—love is love, and will marry in spite of reason, and in some cases it runs away with its choice and repents it a thousand times soon after. But be sensible, for a life contract should be a sensible one. What is the use of throwing away one season—skipping girlhood or boyhood to rush into maturity and maternity? The records of divorce courts tell the silly and sorrowful stories of many a mismated pair, married too young and slowly repenting of their rashness. Ask of your truest friends; take counsel; be above foolishness.

❖

*Don't marry a villain.* Many a girl is ripe for an adventure, and in appearance nothing more resembles an angel than a keen and designing villain—a thoroughbred; not a gambler merely, but worse, a wreck! Such men may be wary, artful, deceitful, attractive. They are crafty; their trade compels it. They may be handsome, often so; they may be oily and slick—most of them are. They may live rich and expensive lives for a season; ill-gotten gains are not lasting. Heaven pity the girl that marries one of these adventurers, for the end is bitterness! A friend met one on the Pacific road, married him, and learned to her sorrow that he drank to excess, swore like a pirate, lived in debauchery, and early offered to swap wives for a season with a boon-companion. "And that man," she said, "was as handsome as a dude, as slick as an auctioneer, as oily as a pedler; I loved him only one day after marriage."

❖

*Don't marry a hypocrite.* Of all things get sincerity. Get the genuine article. If you get a hypocrite, he is brass jewelry, and will easily tarnish. Make careful inquiry, see that he is all that he pretends to be, or never trust him. The habit of deceit is one of a lifetime. Some join churches for no other reason than to cloak iniquity. It is not the rule by any means; it is a too common exception. One who goes from city to city and captivates too many by his oil of blandness; one who has no business, an idler; one who apes the rich and is ground down in poverty; one who lacks the courage to live like himself and had rather live a lie and deceive the world around him—is an unfit companion, and will bear watching.

❖

*Don't marry a coquette.* One that is worn out by a long list of discarded admirers is like stale bread—worse every day and seldom grows better by long standing. There are women, and girls sometimes, who glory and revel in the names of discarded lovers; whose sense of honesty has been poisoned, numbed, and frozen by cheating their victims through pretended affection, until they have lost all heart or honesty; who deserve to be left alone to ponder on their cruelty for the balance of their miserable existence. Of all the worst forms of flirting, coquetry is the most detestable. It is not only trifling away the time of both, but casting distrust on the holiest of all sentiments, the purity of womanhood. To steal money is honorable compared to stealing affection. The habit of coquetry will, or may, last long after marriage. She who practises it will follow up in unpleasant references to her conquests, wishing she had married at this offer or that, and wear out the happiness of her last conquest by a frequent reminder of his inferiority to the others.

❖

*Don't marry a woman for her money.* These people are tenacious to a minute degree. They long to remind you of my house, my property, my farm, my lots on Lincoln Avenue, my furniture, my bank account, and the like—making one a pensioner all his life for his board and clothing. If there is any difference, it should be with the man. He is expected to control property. He is the master of his house, or the manager of his expenses. Very naturally he says "my" store or "my" lots, but it will sound far more fair and considerate even if he says "our" in lieu of "my" sometimes. The only fair way to act about it is to treat marriage as a partnership where nobody owns all, but each has an equal interest. It is fair to divide a good portion of one's property with his wife, fair to deed her a nice homestead and present her a given allowance—liberal as one's income will warrant—and let her draw from it as her own, and not be a beggar each time she needs money.

❖

*Don't elope to marry.* It is a weak affection that cannot wait awhile. Jacob served seven years, then seven more, for Rebecca. She was a fine specimen of womanhood—as represented in paintings; housekeeping was easy and inexpensive then, but they patiently waited and were handsomely rewarded. Ruth was an excellent example of girlhood. In no great hurry to marry, taking the hardships of travel, her devotion to her mother touched the heart of a king, and she won a splendid prize for her patience. She might have eloped with a stage-driver or a coachman, and ended her life with many less historical-society notices.

❖

*Don't dally about proposing.* What is it to ask a fine girl to marry you? The simplest, easiest thing on earth, if you "strike while the iron is hot". Go about it sensibly. To begin with, you never expect much encouragement from a discreet maiden; she is in the background; her promise is to be invited; she is not her own spokeswoman. Think of the embarrassment. I venture to say, if you like her, that you will say so. Often you may have told her how fine her eyes are, or how well you like her singing, or talking, and her company; but when you ask a simple question, you get down on your knees (they do in novels, not in reality) and beg for it. Nonsense! Such a girl is unworthy.

Begging is a silly fashion, seldom now indulged in, all out of date, and no longer tolerated outside of novels and theatres. Use a little sense about it.

Find out first if you have the right one, then settle the matter in one of five ways: First, in the parlor (don't propose in church, or at a donation, or in a crowd, or on a street-car, or while the horse is prancing), get up your resolution at the right moment and say: "Do we understand each other, Clemantha?" Then, if she doesn't, explain it to her in a sensible fashion, and in little short words that cannot be mistaken; give her time, if necessary.

The second way is, on a fine walk or drive, "Would

you like to walk always?" or, "If you were to choose whom you would walk with forever, who would it be?" She will say, "I don't care to be so personal." Certainly then you may be more explicit.

Third, suppose you are to separate, what a grand opportunity! See that you improve it earnestly. To tell a girl that she is fairer than flowers, clearer than coffee, and sweeter than honey is old, very old, and uncalled-for. Tell her she is what she is, and you like her with all her surroundings; that you can better her condition sometime. Dwell on the "sometime".

Be honest about it. If she doesn't love you, let her love some one else, and you will be surprised to find how many pure and beautiful beings there are all around you, holding their finger-tips to hide a smile of welcome and ready—"yes, Edgar"—eager to mate with one worthy and ready to marry them, for marriage is a natural hope of every right-minded woman.

This is a fourth method: read aloud of characters like Arden, Romeo, or Abelard, or Paul and Virginia, and make your comments audibly. You will not be long in tracing a conclusion. Be a little ingenious about it, find out through your sister. Prepare the way and don't ask until you find she is unpledged, remember; or at least tarry long enough to be reasonably certain.

And what if refused? No harm done. Like the German's sugar, "The other pound is shust so good as the first one".

One man I know drew off a list of all his acquaintances worthy of marriage, and went about it like a regular wheat-buyer. He was a bachelor, of course, and very eccentric. Coming to the first, he explained his object, concealing all names, but saying she was first of a long list furnished him by a friend (each one was first, always); then he would say, "I will give you a week to consider it, and no harm done; if not then, I must pursue my list further." Of all the sold-out men, he was sold the cheapest! He married a whole family. The first two were disgusted, the third or fourth accepted. This looks too much like a purchase and sale, and don't try the method.

The last way is sensible; by writing—many a proposal is in writing. Even in that be a little guarded; once a no, yeses come with reluctance. It is best not to give one an opportunity to say no, but to parry long enough to test the opposition. If it were a race-horse to buy, a house to contract for, or a block to purchase, it would not be very hard to strike a bargain. So that, once finding form, character, fitness, affection, desire to be mated, go about the rest by a direct and sensible method, and don't wear out the gate-hinges, burn out all the oil, weary the old folks, or turn gray with anxiety, but do it.

❖

*Don't marry a fast man or woman.* The edge of virtue once dulled is never quite so keen afterwards. It may be very well to speak slightingly of wild oats, but who cares to know that their oats are a second crop? Who is willing to believe that they are the last resort of one who has pleaded and pledged to hundreds or even dozens before her, or waits an opportunity to make as many more pledges as occasion may offer? Fast men are not satisfied with one vice merely, but follow on to many. They may drink, gamble, sport, and venture, and step by step indulge in the kindred vices of lewdness, till disease shall fasten its clutches in their burning blood and run in their veins for a lifetime. They are rarely satisfied with one home, one wife, and one family.

❖

*Don't marry a spendthrift.* The habit of living is formed early. Either one is bent on rising or going lower. As water seeks its level, so men seek their ambition and find it. Prosperity comes not on silver trays, ready-made and ready for use to everybody; most men work for it, strive for it, and deserve it. The sons of the rich, who inherit property and have formed the habit of useless spending, are a little bit lower than the poor. It is not disgraceful at all to be born poor; but to become so after once being rich, and that through reckless spending, is a dishonor to any one. "One thing we can be proud of," said Ingersoll; "we've made some improvement on the original implements and the common stock." A young man who lives on his father's earnings has very little to boast of, but one who squanders his inheritance in riotous living is an object of contempt and ridicule. "He is one of the old man's pensioners," said a business man lately of a rich man's son. "But for his father's thrift he would be a beggar; he lives like a refined beggar on the food furnished by another. What a brilliant genius he is!"

❖

*Don't marry your cousin.* It may be very tempting; relatives are often warmly attached to each other from long and intimate acquaintance. Remember that constantly being thrown in each other's society will often create such attachments. With many persons, marriage of blood relations will more or less lead to deafness, blindness, or deformity. It may skip one generation and find another. It may result in disease and weakness. It may be all right, but seven to eight it is risky and uncertain, and you can't afford to be uncertain in such matters.

❖

*Don't marry too far above or below you.* There is no such thing as station in this country, like the titles and surroundings of Europe; but ignorance mated with refinement must be lost and confused, and ill at ease every hour. Such matches are hasty, and poorly considered. They lead to gossip and resentment of relatives, and an uncomfortable ill-feeling, seldom cured for a full generation. If one has beauty and refinement and is poor, never mind the poverty; the good qualities are more than a balance. But the marriage of a millionaire's daughter with a coachman is supreme folly. It ends in disunion, and never in harmony. Water and oil will as soon mix as such elements. Avoid them.

❖

*Don't marry a doubly divorced man or woman*: it's risky. Something is wrong surely. One divorce should cure any one. Two is a profusion. It may be that the doubly divorced is innocent—he will claim to be; but if he seeks a new party to a possible divorce case (it will be a habit by this time), tell him to wait a little longer. Grass widows may be very lovable creatures, but unless their other halves were clearly blamable, beyond reasonable question, give them a wide road and avoid them entirely. It is a very bad sign, possibly a habit, that a man and woman mate and divide soon after; the fault may belong to either, and most likely relates to both, in similar proportions.

❖

*Don't marry a miser.* Of all the old "curmudgeons" on earth, deliver me from crabbed, narrow-minded, pinch-penny, miserable misers. They begrudge you your meals and clothing. They count your shillings and control your pin purchases; they make life a burden, by owning much and using little, and eternally twit you of every quarter used ever so sparingly. Life is made to live in and enjoy. We make only one journey. We need not open up our purses and leak out the pennies, just to see them roll around promiscuously; but cutting notches on a stick for each one of them, and never spending, even for necessaries, without dread and grudging, is intolerable. I had rather be poor and enjoy something.

❖

*Don't marry too far apart in ages.* June and December is a long, long distance in matrimony. Some people are as young-hearted at sixty as others are at forty. Some men at forty-five have hardly reached their manhood. But old, white-headed men, marrying girls in their teens—servants generally—are pitiable spectacles. To the girl it is suicide; to the man sheer folly; no need of marrying the man. The girl is the most interested in this don't sentence. Why not, if you love him? This is the reason, not jealousy—that is a partial reason—but consistency. Think of a trip round the world or across the continent with one older than your father, to be called your husband, to be your husband! It must be humiliating. It is annoying. It is foolishly silly and inconsistent. Money is a small compensation for such a sacrifice. Love, and love only, should govern marriage, and I doubt its sincerity when the difference goes beyond reason.

Marry one whom you trust, admire, respect, look up to, and confide in, can be true to, and one whom you love from good and earnest motives. "Respect is a cold lunch in a dark dining-room. Love is a picnic in the woods." Think of a picnic and an old man escort!

❖

*Don't marry too old.* Be in earnest about it. Here is the thought in a nut-shell:

### TOO OLD TO LOVE

I.

"I never loved but one," she said;
"I loved him just for fun," she said;
And, saying this, she swung her head—
Had she been frank, they had been wed.
I saw her at a ball that night,
Her eyes so dark and face so white,
Her tone and manner wild delight;
I knew she served him not aright.

II.

"I am too old to love," she said;
"The one I loved in fun is dead!
I plant these flowers above his head,
Here lies my idol, dead!" she said.
"'Tis sad to think it might have been;
'Tis sadder yet to feel my sin.
Love learns too late; but then, but then,
He loved me once—the best of men.

III.

"I never see a pure, good face,
Nor painting outlines ever trace,
But he is near, his love is dear,
Had I been earnest; he were here!"

She veiled her dark eyes with her hand;
I turned away, —"True love is grand,"
I murmured, in an undertone;
"Life gives no more than love of one."

❖

*Don't marry odd sizes.* A tall man with a little woman looks awkward enough; but a tall woman with a little, tiny man is a misfit, surely. See if you can't find someone of your size, as the school-lads say in a wrestle. Pair off like soldiers in time of dress parade, with an eye to unity. This caution relates to extremes, of course, and not to small variances. Some change and grow portly after marriage, but none get very much taller after twenty-four. Just for the looks of the thing, pair off in uniform lines.

❖

*Don't marry a man or woman without a character.* Soon enough you'll see the value of this caution. Character is a matter that grows through a lifetime, but enough of it crops out early to be noticed. One is known not only by his company but by his habits, his tastes, and his inclinations. It is said that some whole families are born fast; some thievish, some inclined to crabbedness, others mild, upright, honest, and reliable. It runs in the blood in some cases. Suppose one is to marry for virtue, purity, and uprightness, he will seek it in the blood as much as he would look for quality in a racer. If a woman loves a rakish "man of the world", so called—a name too often used to varnish a bad character—she will very easily find him around the different bar-rooms of almost any crowded hotel in the city or village. He will be after marriage what he was before. Tell me where a man goes, and I will tell you what he is. If he is fast, he will cultivate fast habits, live a rapid life, and earn that character very early. If these are the traits you are looking for, "inquire within" and you will find them. It may be a woman you are asking about, a girl for a wife, a life-long companion. Which are you seeking for? A dashy, fly-away dancer, or a domestic home-lover, and one whom you can trust with your keys, your secrets, your conscience? Look to her character. In either case, the man or woman has lived somewhere. Find out about it—how long, how well, how faithfully. A well-to-do widow was crazy to marry a man that she fancied, and who actually refused to give more than his name and hotel, and no references. On careful inquiry such a person was known by no less than two to four names—changed to suit circumstances. The spell was broken, the match ended.

Men and women often rush into matrimony as game is run into a trap, for the little tempting bait set to catch them (a catch-as-catch-can race). They marry and risk a life-long happiness on less actual information of each other's real nature than a good horseman would exact of his carriage horse's pedigree. This may do in the country, but never will answer in a city. Sense and reason dictate that men and women, to enjoy each other's society, should see well to the match beforehand. A fine hand, a small foot, a becoming hat, a twist of the head, a simper, or a half-witty saying will do well in their places; but colors must wash and wear to stand a lifetime.

❖

*Don't marry a clown.* A silly fellow that jokes on every subject never did amount to anything, and never will. All he says may be very funny, very; but how many times can he be funny? Fun will grow stale and threadbare; one cannot live by it. Life is a trip that costs car fare, wash bills, board bills, trinkets, notions, and actual outlays. Real providers are never clowns; the clownish fellow is a favorite in school-days. He is so cute, just as cute as a cotton hat, so cunning, so witty, so nice. Is he? Wait a few years, until his nice nonsense turns to active business!

❖

*Don't marry a dude.* Of all milk-and-water specimens, a dude is the lowest—a little removed from nothing; a dressed-up model for a tailor-shop; a street flirt, a hotel-step gazer, an eye-glass ogler, a street strut; one who finds his enjoyment in the looking-glass—a masher. Very many are called, but few are chosen. The many that are called are ridiculed. Men, real men of business, and men fit to marry, are not dudes, but manly, upright beings, with sense, integrity, and genius or industry.

Life is too earnest to spend on silly, tawdry, fancy colors or showy clothing; and the one who has the less of it is the most likely to be marked for a gentleman, and the brand will be correctly designated. With women, no less than men, is this silly street-walking habit quite prevalent. A flirting woman on a public street is a sorry picture; even one who stoops to notice her must secretly know her measure. She deceives no one, for her character, like the dude's, is so transparent that no one mistakes its meaning. The habit of going nowhere for nothing is as foolish as it is injurious. Character grows out of little things. It may be that being seen with a disreputable person three times, or even once, will change the whole current of our career. Don't practise the vices of dudes nor the habits of street flirts.

❖

*Do not marry a boy or girl who is not good at home.* That is the golden test of duty—to do one's duty alone, away from the eyes of men and the notice of the world; to be good from a right disposition. There is no safer rule to marry by than this: "She loves her mother, and isn't afraid to work. She has a good name at home among her near neighbors. She is neat, sweet, and tidy. Seven days each week she is never off guard, always a lady." And of a man may it be said, "He is a man, take him all in all; he is manly, he is truthful; he loves his home; he treats his sisters and mother kindly. He is capable of good deeds, and incapable of mean ones. He has a good name." He deserves success, and it will follow him. He is plain, perhaps, but man outgrows it. He is not a painting, an imitation, a counterfeit, but simply a man. He will do to marry; so will she, the last-named.

❖

*Don't marry from pity*. It may be akin to love, but the kinship is quite distant. Many a weak woman has so married, and only once regretted it—each and every day afterwards. A life-long regret must follow. What a cold respect is that compliment to any woman, "I took pity on her!" Away with such base uses of pity!

Many a woman has had pity on a rakish man or a drunkard and married him to reform his nature. Better, far better, trust a child with a runaway horse or a mad dog. Danger seen and not avoided is criminal carelessness. Surely you can save one life, and its happiness, in such cases. One is quite enough to be sacrificed. Let bravery be shown by demanding a full surrender and reasonable atonement.

❖

*Don't marry for an ideal marriage only.* The girlish dream of marriage is so wide of the reality as to be dangerous. She is to grow up and go away, off to Italy, or some far-away clime of sunshine; there to be taught music and the classics. On some clear moonlit evening, in a summer-time, where birds sing all day long, near a brook or flower-garden, she is to be surprised by a creature of form and make and mental endowment that shall thrill her whole being into rapturous joy. They will go to the parlor, and there, by a grand-piano, she will unseal the pent-up currents of her heart, till tears flow from all eyes around her; there she will seem to hear the childhood melodies, the song of departed friends, the harmony of all the senses, mingling in one sweet welcome to her new-found happiness. Her prisoned soul is no longer grovelling in common themes; all the latent power of her being is to burst forth in gladness; and music of the heart is to bear her up until the cottage walls are narrow, till flowers and falling water, brilliant company, ease and riches, smile upon her glad career. She is to be lifted up, and raised to heights before unknown to mortals. He of whom she dreams now is fit for Paradise. Finer and finer every day will his genius grow, and nearer to her liking every hour. There is just such joy and just such glory in a new-born love, that seems to reach a grander height each moment, as on eagle's wings. And this is but the generous dream that Nature gives, as a preface to a real life after—so very, very different. The girl that twines her tender arms around her mother's neck, and thrills with joyous pride in telling of the brilliant prize that's offered her, thinks not of rainy days ahead. Perhaps it is just as well; who would begrudge her such half-hours of happiness? But, seeing sometime she must break the spell and know all, it may be safe to drop a hint in season, and say, This way lies safety, that way danger!

❖

*Don't marry a man of even doubtful character.*

No matter how handsome or brilliant, a bad

man has in him elements that are always repulsive; they are poison to his blood and his surroundings, and the only safe guide is his character. No matter how many promises of reformation; you need not turn reformer for his sake. If you will take the risk, do it after he proves himself reformed, and be in no great haste about it. No amount of spicing and seasoning can make tainted meat palatable, and no amount of promising will reclaim a character tainted with vicious habits once seated. Young ladies who enter upon the reforming mission furnish more women and children for prisons, later in life, by their own misfortunes than any one class. Cases of reclaimed men after marriage are so rare as to be exceptional. It's always a dangerous experiment.

❖

*Don't marry too cautiously as to perfection.* It has before been fully stated that men and women are human, and imperfect. That is, if you are hunting angels it's a fool's errand; there are none unpledged. If you look for tall, handsome, rich, manly, cultivated, talented, brilliant men, or pure, refined, fascinating, beautiful women, and one for each man the world over, the supply never equals the demand of either sex. But to presume that the persons marked under head of "don't marry" cover all the rest is unreasonable. There are thousands of noble women and men, possessed of sterling sense, strong bodies, affectionate natures, ability to conduct a home, become a genial companion, raise a family, shine in society, and bear their full share of life's earnest work. Occasionally a man or woman will tower above their fellows, but, generally, the real difference is less than is often supposed. The great majority are good, and live and go to their reward unheard of outside of their neighborhood.

One has put it rather strongly in this, to many: "The lives of men and women, the best of them, are marred and ruined by uncongenial marriages. They mostly suffer in silence, ashamed to complain of the chain they cannot break. Men and woman cannot know what their sweethearts will be after marriage. I have known a sensitive man, a genius with a soul like a star, whose life was a pilgrimage over burning coals, because his wife was a coarse termagant. Many a gifted woman, fit to be a queen or an empress, is chained to a clod of a husband, whose forced companionship is to her the tortures of Inferno."

❖

*Don't marry expecting all the virtues in one person.* If you do, the disappointment will be startling. There are no perfect characters. History gives none since the Saviour. Even Joseph was willing to punish his enemies. The majority of men and women are good and pure and fair-looking. The numbers who go to the bad are few compared to the good. Take the country population, and ninety per cent will be good; and sixty per cent of all cities are people of fair characters. It is a mistake to think that most people are bad because the bad ones get so often chronicled in public journals. The good, like the virtuous, live and die and demand no praise of their virtue. The great mass of men are sensible, and honest and upright and sober, and worthy to marry.

❖

*Don't break a marriage abruptly.* This is the wrong way to break a bad match. It intensifies affection. It leads to elopement, or that slow canker in a girl's nature ending in melancholy, or insanity. Love is a plant so tender that to uproot or transplant it may touch a vital part. There are ways enough to change its current; but of all food to increase its growth, give it a little opposition. Tell a child to leave something alone, and he sulks to touch it. Tell a girl that the man she admires is distasteful to her relatives, and she half despises them from a simple motive of resentment. Lead her by reason to see with her own eyes, and she will be convinced. The great London actor, Garrick, played the drunkard to disenchant a girl, and succeeded. Her parents might have tried it a lifetime and failed. Human nature is queer. It will lead when the way is enticing. It will magnify discoveries, but they must be discovered in the right manner. Remove not the prop till the safety of the structure is secure without it.

❖

*Don't oppose one's marriage choice suddenly.* Should a girl fall in love with one of bad character, it is best not to call him so at one breath; but say, "What are his habits? Is he good enough and worthy of so pure and comely a person as you are?" Let this task be performed by some girl of the same age and class as the one you seek to change. Let them be often together, and find ways of expressing the objections by this method—coming from a classmate, a friend, a chum or companion—and your object may be easily accomplished. A proposed absence without showing why, a long journey with genial company, may have the desired effect. At least use one caution; see that the girl knows the real habits and character of the man you are opposed to her marrying. It will do more than all the urging, scolding, coaxing, or threatening.

❖

*Don't marry for spite.* Why should you? If the one whom you loved most has deceived you and taken another, it will be folly to try to punish him by hanging yourself, or committing a double suicide in a loveless marriage. You will learn this lesson all too dearly when it's over. Life is too short for those who love it and are well mated; but many a miserable marriage has made one or the other wish for death a million times, to be rid of its burden. You are the one most interested. You will find out, after the knot is tied, that there are many conditions in life better and easier to be endured than a silly marriage to spite some one. You will spite them better by showing what a noble choice they had missed when they took another in your place.

❖

*Don't propose on a wash-day, in the rain, at breakfast, or in a tunnel.* There is no room for fainting in the former, and a narrow chance for time in the latter. Many ladies have singular notions on how proposals should be accepted, and to such any rudeness is extremely shocking. A very modest fellow, in deep anxiety, took up his fair lady's cat, and said, "Pussy, may I marry your mistress?" when the young lady replied, "Say yes, pussy, when he gets brave enough to ask for her." More than likely this brought the young fellow to his senses. It certainly brought matters to a crisis. Most young people talk to each other as though a tall stone wall stood between them and they must find a door in it. Strange enough, the difference in views vanishes at the merest mention of each other's sentiments.

❖

*Don't mitten a mechanic, simply on account of his business.* If he is worthy, never mind his business. He can grow out of it, and will grow out of it. Collier was a blacksmith, Wilson a shoemaker, Andrew Johnson a tailor, Peter Cooper a glue-maker, Grant a tanner, and Lincoln the humblest of farmers. In this country it is not a question what a man was, but what he is; not even what he is, but what he may be, and what he is capable of yet attaining. Many a girl has turned away a mechanic and married a rich loafer, only to find in good season that the mechanic was at heart a gentleman, with growing possibilities, and the loafer remained such for all time.

Advice is seldom heeded in such matters, but it may do to mention it. The true test of manhood is seen in the mettle of boyhood. If you wish to forecast the future, study the past history of your subject. If one is selfish, tyrannical, and overbearing by being rich, he will be a bad man to marry. If, on the other hand, he is pleasant, kind, genial, and forbearing, loves his kind, is attentive to his mother and sisters, and has made friends and character in early life, he is not very likely to change his notions later. There is often more manhood in a poor one-armed man than a rich athlete.

❖

*Don't marry a man too poor.* It is the height of folly to mate, and attempt to raise seven children on what will bring up three indifferently. Have a little discretion. Think that eating, dressing, etc., cost something, and no one can live happily without some of these common comforts. If they cannot buy them single, it is folly to double one's misery by marrying in the jaws of starvation. It is suicide: it is worse—it is double suicide, and may lead to pauperism and crime and disgrace.

❖

*Don't marry where the woman is older than the man.* Men are restless creatures and exacting. They expect grace, beauty, and refinement; they prefer youth to age, generally. At least it is the fashion to marry a wife some years younger than the husband. Women mature earlier; they have less expectancy of long life, and on an average live seven to ten years less, and show age at fifty more than a man does at sixty-five. Of the two, a woman should look smaller and younger and better than a man. This accords with the belief of all refined people.

❖

*Don't marry a crank.* This class of men will be wordy and persuasive. They tell all sorts of stories of life—how the world is mismade; how they could improve upon this thing or that; how marriages should be made between blondes and brunettes; how, with their philosophy, society would reach perfection. Such men are invariably tyrannical. They are exacting to the last degree; they have neither faith, hope, nor charity, but run in one groove. They distrust the powers that be, and generally mount some hobby, and forever prattle about the rights of free love or the wrongs of government. Avoid them as you would a tramp.

❖

*Don't marry fine feathers.* Chesterfield was well up on manners, and gave his son this rule, among his twenty-one maxims to marry by: "Let not the rustling of silk entrap you into matrimony." Fine clothing has a certain fascination to many. Some choose a wife by the becoming effect of a tasty garment. Some select a fine dancer; others rely upon a small hand or a petite form. These points may be all well noted, but they are but parts of a greater whole that should govern a wise selection.

❖

*Don't marry a "masher"—man or woman.* A regular professional flirt will never settle down to love one woman or one man. Habits once formed will cling to them in after-life. They are like runaway teams—liable to take fright and go when least expected. Civil attention, by a lady or gentleman, to the other sex is natural and courteous, but the thought that every fair lady is common prey is repulsive.

❖

*Don't marry without love.* It will be plain enough after a while. You will not mind it at first, perhaps, but the time will come when, by a song, or a face, or a voice, or a form, you will awake as from a dream, to find you have hosen carelessly. It will be too late then. A loveless marriage may stand throughout a honeymoon. It may last in youth, but not when storms and trials come in after-years. It lacks that something which words do not well express—continuity, heart-bound devotion, and endurance. No matter how plain each or either may be, if they love each other they will overlook little things, and live patiently and happily to the end. But once, at least, must come this joy and glory of wedlock, that seems to be the wise design of Nature—a love for one another. It endures through age and trouble, and is a more lasting tie than all others together.

❖

*Don't marry an idle spendthrift*; one whose money comes without effort at first, and goes as rapidly, will one day come to want as certainly as waters reach their level. Nature has fashioned us all for work—work of mind or work of body, mental or physical labor—and with it comes strength of muscle and of will. Listless life of idleness, without motive, without aim, is open to every form of temptation. It is not a crime to be rich, or to be poor. It is a crime to be listless in a busy world. He would be disgraced who, standing on a wharf, saw a drowning crew without offering relief. He would be a coward who would not defend a woman in distress; yet all around us are the needy, helpless, drowning, starving, whom it is our duty to rescue and lift up in life; and marriage is the place where society is born, and grows and ripens into use.

❖

*Don't marry a stingy man*; of all narrow, mean men, he is worst who has money, and has no will to do good with it. A "dog-in-the-manger" man, who can improve his town, his church, his neighborhood, and does not, is a drone in life's hive and deserves no success. One who is poor and has no means is excusable; one who locks and buries treasures deserves the Bible sentence of him who hid his talent in the earth—to be taken from him and placed with the active one's talent. A narrow, selfish, stingy man will count your pennies spent, and postage used, and clothing worn, as wasted. One must live in constant dread of such a creature—we need not name him man; it would disgrace the term. A miser's wife lives a loveless life.

❖

*Don't marry too hastily.* Some rush into matrimony like a steam-engine going to put out a fire, as though one moment lost would be eternal defeat, and the first there gain the highest prize. Many a one has repented more leisurely and in sorrow for such conduct. But of all things, marry at a good opportunity.

❖

*Don't be too slow about it.* Girls who give up the society of all but one, and turn their homes into special receptions for one person, will be worried to death in a year or two, if things move too moderately. Brace up and proceed to business, or release your claim and let some one else have an opportunity. Long engagements lead to lovers' quarrels; they, in turn, fail to make up sometimes, and then follow scandal and gossip over broken ties; and later two go down to their early sleep disheartened, ruined by a trifling neglect and a reasonable inventory of prospects. You will see it all plainly when it is over. It will be a "might have been" then, sure enough, but too late.

❖

*Don't marry a silly girl.* It's something of an art to select a sensible person, but many are captivated by frivolous sayings and coquettish acts of simpering school-girls and marry them. They make better playmates than wives. They are generally shallow, nonsensical, and superficial. They seldom learn anything; a tittering girl is wearisome in real life. They are ever unstable as water and changeable as wind; get some one that you can rely upon in confidence.

❖

*Avoid slovenly dressed girls or heedless men.* Life seems very short sometimes, but if ill-mated it may be a long and tiresome life. A woman with shoes run down, a man with slouched and battered hat, reckless of neatness, will grow worse, and seldom better. Trifling as it may appear, the tidy dress, the tasty every-day apparel, the ladylike appearance, and general style of man or woman, go a long way to form character. Beecher was right in saying that "clothes do not make the man, but they make him look better after he is made." The same rule is true of women.

❖

*Don't expect too much in marriage.* The story pen-pictures and fashion-plate models of men that we see and read about are always exaggerated.

Not one man in a million would equal their description. Men are plain flesh-and-blood creatures; women are not angels. They build their hopes too high who expect otherwise. Take the handsomest person you know and ten years' wear will dull the edges; and of all faded features, the once very handsome show change the soonest. There are many little odd-faced fellows who grow up to be fine manly men. The growth from boyhood or girlhood to youth, and youth to manhood or womanhood, and so on to old age, is marvellous. It takes a keen sense of foresight to measure the future of many boys and girls by their beginning. There is no rule safer than choosing a good form, a good brain, a good temper, and a good character, and waiting for the other developments.

Endure what cannot be cured, and don't wish your wife or husband were as handsome as some neighbor. Youth and good qualities are riches. It may be he is richer by far than the very one envied. The richest are not always those who own the most—many of these are poor indeed, and often miserable.

❖

*Don't expect everything of one person.* Some expect to marry love, beauty, talent, riches, and affection all in one. It is unreasonable;

you will never find it, and may as well give up looking in good season. "Waukeen" Miller was requested to rewrite an article sent to a New York magazine and returned this pithy reply: "I can't re-copy it. I can't do everything. What do you expect of a man, anyway—to be a genius, an inventor, and a writing-teacher? No, I can't bother my brains with copying worth four to six hundred a year at the highest." This covers the whole subject in a sentence. But it is well to add that Nature is sparing of her gifts. To one she allots beauty, to another strength, to another wisdom, to a third courage, to a fourth ability to acquire riches, to another that to write and speak, to teach, to manage, to paint, or to control armies: all are not alike, and to no one belong all virtues.

❖

*Don't expect too much of a wife.* If she is beautiful, that will be her pride and ideal. If plain, she may make it up a thousand times in goodness, gentleness, industry, virtue (the plainest are the least tempted). Earnest in her duty, she may be of all women the most suited to your station. If talented, she will devote herself to it. You cannot own beauty, talent, domestic drudgery all in one. "Looking for angels, are you?" said an advanced maiden in the country. "Well, you'll not find 'em fit for kitchen work; and, while I think of it, how would you look by the side of an angel, you brute you?" and he subsided. No, they are not much suited to kitchen work, the so-called angels; but many a mother who has brought up a large family as her own kitchen maid, without servants, who has braved the hardships of poverty and privation, has led a life but little lower than the angels, after all.

❖

*Don't marry and cross your husband.* While on this division, don't cross your wife just at dinner-time. After the cares of business he is tired, fretful, and she is of similar humor. To make a dispute is much easier than to make a coal fire. Wait! Don't flash up and speak back, and irritate by quick answer. Wait! If man or woman could only wait in seasons of anger, all would blow over and harmony return like spring flowers, that are not always in blossom. Don't both speak at once, nor both get angry at once, nor both be too determined at once. No one is ever convinced by angry tones. It is horribly repulsive to talk so; besides, you will both be sorry for it very many times. Wait, and let your judgment mature after dinner; quarrel, if you must, in whispers; that is the new fashion. Try the newer form.

About ten thousand new divorces could be prevented each year by observing these rules of common sense and reason. When will married people and unmarried people, and lovers and neighbors, learn how pleasant peace is, and how awkward it is to quarrel together? One man pounds his finger with a tack-hammer and blames his wife for it a month later; one man's goose gets in a neighbor's garden and is killed—perhaps served him right—and yet they are sworn enemies for five years later; and not until some child is rescued from a burning building or a mad dog by the enemy neighbor do the two know how pleasant and useful it is to dwell in harmony.

Families who have been estranged for years are some day—ah, some day!—called to look into the sightless eyes that once flashed in anger, or lay away in its earthy home the form they shunned for some trifling answer in a passion. If we knew how soon, how cautious we would be! Life is so short to quarrel and make up in; they who quarrel may never make up.

❖

*Don't marry in fun.* Be in earnest about a matter of so much moment. It may seem funny to a lot of girls out on a sleigh-ride to call in some one and wind up an escapade by a double wedding; but few of such marriages ever end well. Sudden and ill-considered matches are mismatches. You may have a mother, a sister, or a family to consult; then the old-fashioned way is the best. It's a left-handed marriage at best that will not allow the forms used for ages to strengthen its solemnity. Let the world know by open dealing that you have married above any secrecy, elopement, or underhanded fashion. Be brave enough to follow the form of society in a manner that concerns every neighbor and every relative. Marry at home or at church, in good form, without display; marry according to the best usage of the best people, and you will reap some benefit from the sensible conclusion.

❖

*Don't marry without an eye to comfort.* A man that expects to live thirty years or more with a partner will investigate his likes and dislikes; so should a woman. Are you ready to attend a cattle ranch and brave the frontier? Then look the matter clearly in the face at the first hint of the man's proposal who expects it. Do you prefer the city to the country? Look to the earliest opportunity. Can you endure a soldier's absence, or wait for an explorer? Or will you prefer a domestic relation that brings you both under one roof daily? These questions should be answered soon enough to prevent regret, remorse, or separation. The greatest of all dangers in marriage is the color-blindness of lovers: they never use but one color—rose color—till a few weeks after the wedding.

❖

*Don't spurn a man for his poverty.* "Prosperity is the parent of friends; misfortune is the fire by which they are tried." One may be poor by an honest failure, another may be rich on ill-gotten gains. The first the lord of honor, the last a prosperous knave. "I would give it all willingly and work by the day if we could be placed back where we were, and be free from the worry and dread and anxiety," said a rich man's wife to a waiting friend by her sick bedside. Who does not know of poor, plain boys who endured the poverty of youth, struggled with their studies, carved out a fortune as from flinty marble, and enjoyed it in maturer years, all the more for the effort it cost them, all the more likely to last and continue to bless other generations? Franklin commenced poor with a penny loaf; Greeley was homely and awkward. Few would have looked for Lincoln's rise. Giddings and Collier and Garfield all started low on the ladder, and ended high in honor and worthy of any woman's affection.

If we could only get near enough to Genius to

comprehend its superior worth; if we could reverence talent and admire integrity and take true measure of prospective greatness, what a fortune we would possess! Like high-priced lots in large cities, the discoverers of rare locations seldom knew the value of their purchases. It takes time for development; more time in genius and character than we are always ready to wait for; but the far-seeing are always rewarded, so with the prizes of matrimony.

❖

*Don't marry and expect a husband to be wealthy while young.* Only the older men should be looked to for high financial standing. In a hopeful country like ours, few are rich under fifty, seldom under sixty. Young men who earn their education, and begin and learn a business are barely partners at thirty or thirty-five. It takes time to prosper. Several mistakes may be made. Scarcely a wholesale house in New York or Boston has run on twenty years without a failure. Failure is the rule, success the exception. Patience, pluck, and perseverance win the victory, but they who spend freely in the forenoon have little left in the evening. Those who save early double in like ratio later on.

❖

*Don't marry in opposite religious views.* If possible, marry near your own belief. This may seem strained, but the story of divorces will confirm its wisdom. Children and parents very often disagree on religious subjects. The farmer's "Betsey and I are out" controversy, "was a difference in our creed. And the more we argued the matter, the less we ever agreed." It is pleasant to agree on a subject so vital in families, more especially so in Protestant and Catholic families, where education is some times controlled by church government, and marriages are held illegal in one church if not solemnized by its forms and between regular believers in its faith and doctrines.

❖

*Don't marry a duke, or any man who travels on his title.* The most of such men are very common, and the most of young people who seek their company are sold, deceived, and seriously disappointed. They expect a fortune to begin with, and will be the most exacting of all mortals. This is a mere matter of birth and surroundings. Novels tell many beautiful stories (pretty visions) about brave and noble dukes and their princely palaces, attentive servants, and flower-arbors. Experience tells far different stories.

The history of nine out of ten of such unnatural unions is a record of a half million or so squandered on a petted daughter to satisfy a mother's ambition, and ending in misery entailed by the dearly bought purchase. Don't marry so much out of rank as to be a burden, or carry a burden.

❖

*Do marry a man that you can look up to*, and see that he can do likewise. There are plenty of farmers, mechanics, merchants, conductors, doctors, lawyers, and men of general business, who are worthy, trusty, generous, noble, and will make excellent husbands. Seek them out from their character, their conduct at home, their treatment of sisters and mothers, their devotion to business and adherence to principle. Show them that you trust them. Be ready to marry. Become accomplished and useful. Make yourself worthy of a home, and know how to manage it with skill and kindness. Loving natures are not long neglected.

❖

*Do marry a President.* That is the correct form now. It's so romantic. Waive all the hints of other objections—age, love, spite, money, and the like. Get a President—just for the position, you know! Then all the little jewels and diamonds and presents will come rolling in like flowers to a favorite singer. All little objections vanish in the presence of a President. He must be suited to any condition of beauty, genius, or intellect. Don't refuse a President's offer; you may never get but one such in a lifetime.

❖

*Do marry a plain man.* Just a plain, common-sense man; be he banker, lawyer, doctor, farmer, builder, merchant, so he is a man; for manhood is at a premium to-day in home life! The world is full to overflowing with brilliant men. Public offices are public trusts, and all that such responsibility implies, and there are women in stations where the word home has very little meaning, and other women who long for the quiet and comfort of true domestic life away from the cares of office and the demands of lofty stations. Two of the things that lead to greatest misery of the masses to-day are over-ambition and reckless marriages.

❖

*Don't coax a woman to love you.* If you wish to win, that is certainly the wrong way. If they have any notion of it, you are in the opposite direction of success. Women despise a fawning, cringing nature. A far more sensible way to win will be by indifference. Show enough willingness to reassure her, and enough courage to act manly. Ten to one you have mistaken her temper by lack of frankness. Nothing is more touching than truth. If you are really bent on marrying and have told the right person the whole story, earnestly and truthfully, the answer should be decisive. Keen dealers seldom banter; they may hesitate, they may explain their wants and wishes, they never parley very long or express much anxiety to strike a bargain.

❖

*Winning a wife or a lover is a rare art.* To be worthy of either is the first essential. It is better to be worthy of it than to be President and unworthy. It must be consoling even to a jilted lover to feel that he is superior to the one successful. The next thing to being worthy is being ready. Many a youth begins driving, sleighing, and dressing for society who pays his clothing bills by instalments, and whose salary is wholly unequal to his outlay. Fairness demands that a girl in marrying should better her condition. How can one expect her to marry into misery? Chesterfield quotes an old Spanish saying of great force and aptness: "It is the beginning that costs in everything. The first step over, the rest is easy."

❖

*Don't marry recklessly.* Before two or more men form a partnership, they learn each other's means of furthering the business to be engaged in; the confidence that each is worthy of, the skill, attention, etc., each can give, and the prospects of a mutual agreement and prosperity. Without some inquiry on these vital requisites, no company concern would be founded. It would be a foolish investment to purchase goods and fit up stores or warehouses without some forecast of results; and yet this is precisely in the line of marriage.

Partnerships are business marriages. It is not

best to be too cool and calculating about it; one caution may let another take the venture and draw the premium. But some common-sense may as well be mixed with a matter so vital as a life-long engagement. Firms are limited to a few years; marriages are unlimited save by death, or divorce, for over a third of a century, on an average. While it is very difficult to tell whom to marry—for no one can foresee your circumstances—still, it is well to mention a large class that no one should marry, at least till all others are no longer accessible.

If one could foresee the extent of happiness depending on this selection of partners, if he would take a simple business caution and investigate enough to be considerate, he might save society from disgrace and himself from lasting misery. For the fact is, that the most glaring of all our American evils is the looseness of marriage ties, and the misery it entails on domestic relations. If these hints or reminders should induce one woman to avoid a bad marriage, and one man to contract a good one, or save a long quarrel, or keep families in harmony, or help some poor bashful fellow to gain his Yes by a sensible proposal, the time in reading will be well spent, the trifling cost will be a splendid investment.

•1891•